THE SCARIEST PLACES ON EARTH
EDINBURGH CASTLE

BY NICK GORDON

BELLWETHER MEDIA · MINNEAPOLIS, MN

Are you ready to take it to the extreme?
Torque books thrust you into the action-packed world
of sports, vehicles, mystery, and adventure. These
books may include dirt, smoke, fire, and chilling tales.
WARNING : read at your own risk.

Library of Congress Cataloging-in-Publication Data

Gordon, Nick.
Edinburgh Castle / by Nick Gordon.
    pages cm. -- (Torque : the scariest places on earth)
Includes bibliographical references and index.
Summary: "Engaging images accompany information about Edinburgh Castle. The combination of high-
interest subject matter and light text is intended for students in grades 3 through 7"--Provided by publisher.
ISBN 978-1-60014-948-1 (hardcover : alk. paper)
1. Haunted castles--Scotland--Edinburgh--Juvenile literature. 2. Ghosts--Scotland--Edinburgh--Juvenile
literature. 3. Edinburgh Castle (Edinburgh, Scotland)--Miscellanea--Juvenile literature. 4. Edinburgh
Castle (Edinburgh, Scotland)--History--Juvenile literature. I. Title.
BF1474.G67 2014
133.1'294134--dc23
                                                            2013009633

This edition first published in 2014 by Bellwether Media, Inc.

Printed in the United States of America, North Mankato, MN.

TABLE OF CONTENTS

CHAPTER 1

A GHOSTLY ENCOUNTER

Your footsteps echo through the halls of Edinburgh Castle. In the distance, you hear the **eerie** sound of **bagpipes**. Suddenly, you feel a tug at your shirt. You turn around and jump. A dark shadow passes in front of you. Are you sure you are ready to take on a haunted castle?

CHAPTER 2

A VERY OLD CASTLE

Edinburgh Castle is a huge **fortress**. It towers over the city of Edinburgh, Scotland. Parts of the castle have stood for 900 years. It was a key location in wars between Scotland and England in the 1300s. It was also home to many kings and queens of Scotland.

CASTLE ROCK

Edinburgh Castle stands on Castle Rock. Millions of years ago, this rock was part of a volcano.

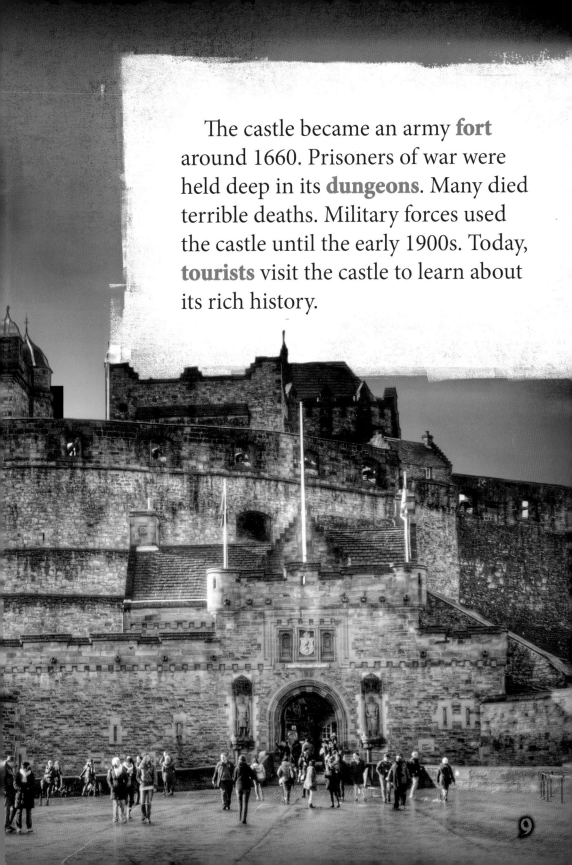

The castle became an army **fort** around 1660. Prisoners of war were held deep in its **dungeons**. Many died terrible deaths. Military forces used the castle until the early 1900s. Today, **tourists** visit the castle to learn about its rich history.

CHAPTER 3

RESTLESS SPIRITS

People have seen and heard strange things at Edinburgh Castle for hundreds of years. In 1650, the castle was about to be attacked. Just before the battle, Scottish soldiers heard the sound of drums. Some saw a headless drummer boy. The ghostly drummer returns any time the castle is in danger.

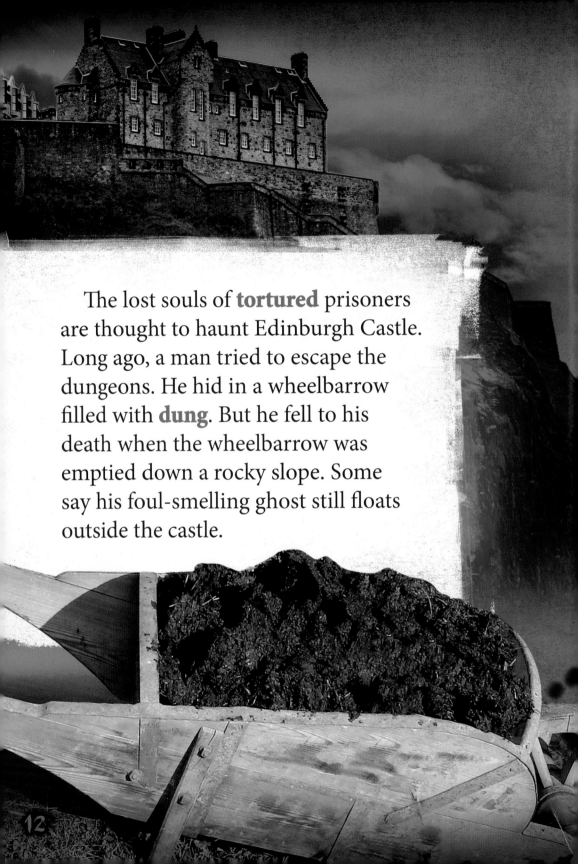

The lost souls of **tortured** prisoners are thought to haunt Edinburgh Castle. Long ago, a man tried to escape the dungeons. He hid in a wheelbarrow filled with **dung**. But he fell to his death when the wheelbarrow was emptied down a rocky slope. Some say his foul-smelling ghost still floats outside the castle.

13

THE PIPER

Hundreds of years ago, tunnels were discovered beneath the castle. A piper was sent to explore them. He played his bagpipes so others could hear him from above. Soon his music faded away. The piper was never seen again. Sometimes visitors can hear the sound of his pipes rising from the tunnels.

Visitors to Edinburgh Castle have also heard the ghost of Lady Jane Douglas. She was punished for practicing **witchcraft** in 1537. The king had her burned to death outside the castle. Some say they hear her crying ghost as it roams the castle grounds.

BLOODY GEORGE

George Mackenzie was a judge in the 1600s. He got the nickname "Bloody Mackenzie" because he loved to sentence criminals to death.

Edinburgh

The ghosts of Edinburgh are not only found within the castle walls. The entire city seems to be haunted. The spirit of Sir George Mackenzie is one of the most troublesome ghosts. The Mackenzie **Poltergeist** is blamed for fires and attacks on more than 400 people. Some **victims** have suffered serious injuries.

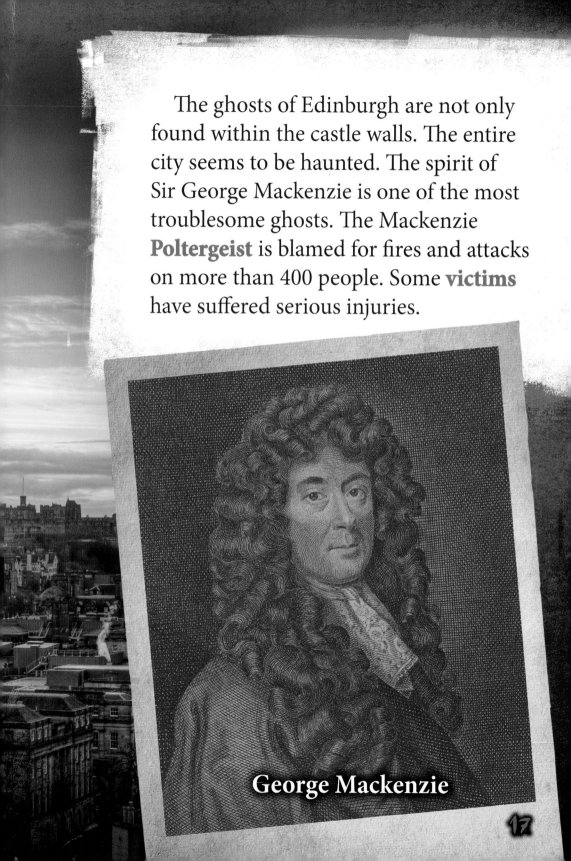

George Mackenzie

REAL OR IMAGINED?

More than one million tourists visit Edinburgh Castle every year. Many look out for ghostly activity. They listen for the faint sound of bagpipes or drums. Some claim to hear it. But is the music coming from ghosts that will not leave? At Edinburgh Castle, it can be tough to know what is real and what is imagined.

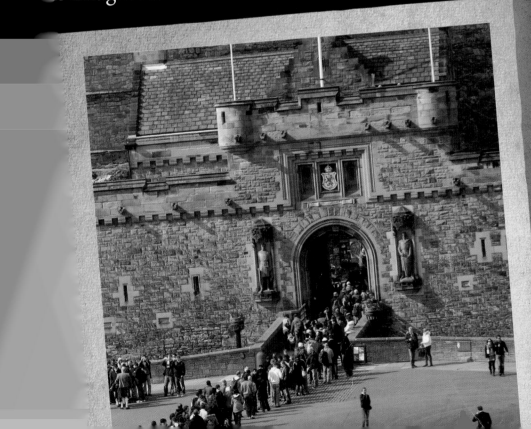

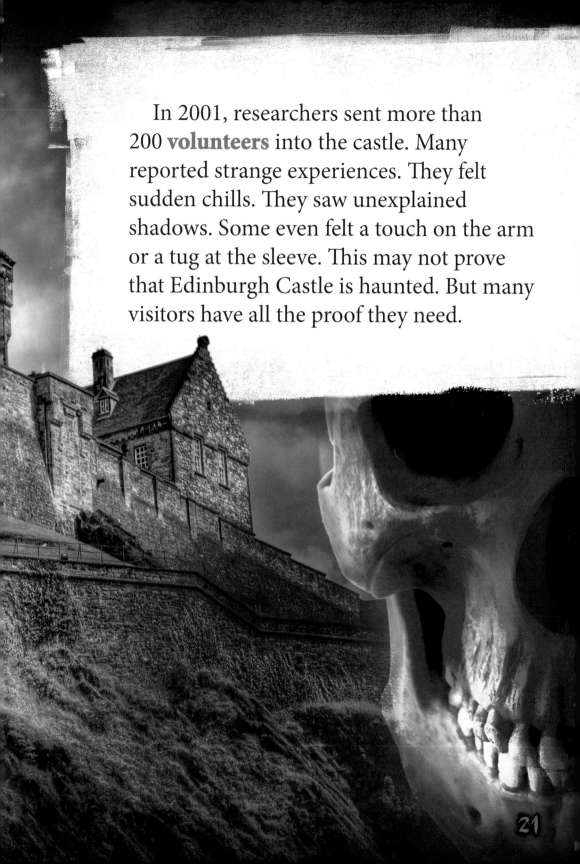

In 2001, researchers sent more than 200 **volunteers** into the castle. Many reported strange experiences. They felt sudden chills. They saw unexplained shadows. Some even felt a touch on the arm or a tug at the sleeve. This may not prove that Edinburgh Castle is haunted. But many visitors have all the proof they need.

GLOSSARY

bagpipes—a Scottish instrument played by squeezing air from a bag and through a set of pipes

dung—animal waste

dungeons—groups of underground rooms in which prisoners are held

eerie—strange and scary

fort—a military post

fortress—a strong building that cannot be easily entered or attacked

poltergeist—an evil spirit that is destructive or violent

tortured—forced to suffer extreme pain

tourists—people who travel to visit another place

victims—people who are hurt, killed, or made to suffer

volunteers—people who offer to do something for free

witchcraft—the use of magic and spells

TO LEARN MORE

AT THE LIBRARY

Hawkins, John. *Hauntings*. New York, N.Y.: PowerKids Press, 2012.

Knox, Barbara. *Edinburgh Castle: Scotland's Haunted Fortress*. New York, N.Y.: Bearport Pub., 2007.

Parvis, Sarah E. *Creepy Castles*. New York, N.Y.: Bearport Pub., 2008.

ON THE WEB

Learning more about Edinburgh Castle is as easy as 1, 2, 3.

1. Go to www.factsurfer.com.

2. Enter "Edinburgh Castle" into the search box.

3. Click the "Surf" button and you will see a list of related Web sites.

With factsurfer.com, finding more information is just a click away.

INDEX